voices voi vo

QUARTERLY ESSAYS ON RELIGION I

CW00549078

Islam, Christianity and the Secular State

❖❖❖❖❖

johngarrattpublishing

FRANK PURCELL

Published in Australia by
John Garratt Publishing
32 Glenvale Crescent
Mulgrave Vic 3170

www.johngarratt.com.au

Islam, Christianity and the Secular State is part of *Voices*, a series of quarterly essays on religion in Australia. The editor, Garry Eastman, welcomes proposals from writers. Write to garryeastman@johngarratt.com.au .

ISSN 1835 6818

First published 2009

Copyright © 2009 Frank Purcell

All rights reserved. Except as provided by Australian copyright law, no part of this book may be reproduced without permission from the publisher.

Designed and typeset by Lynne Muir

Text edited by Cathy Oliver

Print co-ordinated by Advent Print Management

National Library of Australia Cataloguing-in-Publication entry

Purcell, Frank, 1931-
Islam, Christianity and the secular state / Frank Purcell.
ISBN: 9781920721916 (pbk)
Series: Voices v. 2, no. 4
Notes: Bibliography.
Subjects: Religion and sociology—Australia.Religion and politic—Australia.
Islam and state—Australia. Church and state—Australia.
201.70994

Contents

1 RELIGION AND AUSTRALIAN SOCIETY

The relationship between religion and politics has been a cause of tension in Australian society from the time of settlement in 1788. Catholic and Dissenter convicts were forced to attend Anglican church services; a century-long struggle over State Aid for Catholic schools saw Australian society continue until the 1960s that destructive sectarianism which was the legacy of the post-Reformation religious intolerance towards Catholics in Britain and Ireland.

In spite of this on-going religious tension, Australians generally underestimate the crucial role played by Christianity, including Catholicism, in the development of Australian society. We also lack a strong consensus on the proper relationship of religion to public life. There is some confusion among believers and there is the very negative stance of doctrinaire secularists in Australian political life, academia and the media who want religion marginalised and restricted to the private life of each individual. Christians and Muslims who insist that religion does have a role in the public life even of a secular democracy contest those views. Because of the nature of the missionary dimension of religion in Christianity and Islam, a lack of consensus on the proper relationship with civil authorities will pose serious challenges for Australia in maintaining our socially cohesive, multicultural society. Ignoring the role of religion in public life is to ignore the elephant in the room.

Australia's cultural diversity and social harmony

Since the beginning of European settlement Australia has been culturally part of Western civilisation. In spite of the failures in our treatment of our

Indigenous people, and our discriminatory White Australian migration policy, Australian society has been for its non-Aboriginal, largely Anglo-Celtic people, a fairly well-functioning, politically stable, cohesive community.

After the ending of the White Australia policy in 1960s, this country adopted a non-discriminatory migration policy which rejected racial and religious criteria for its selection of migrants while still seeking their integration into Australian society.

We moved from a policy of assimilating migrants into our dominant Anglo-Celtic culture, to one of multiculturalism, in which migrants are not expected to abandon those traditions of their own which do not clash with Australian customs and values. But they are expected to accept certain values and institutions which are the basis of our social cohesion.

Social cohesion comes from that fundamental understanding within a community on how we expect one another to live and work together. There are certain basic rules we all accept and try to live by. Those rules flow from a mixture of a shared acceptance of certain universal principles, the way we interpret them and the patterns of behaviour that flow from them. And, of course, that understanding changes and evolves with new experiences. New insights into the human condition result in revised visions of equality and fairness. But at any particular time we all know that certain kinds of behaviour are just not acceptable. If that kind of behavior happens too often, our social cohesion is at risk because something almost sacred has been violated.

All migrants to Australia, earlier arrivals as well as the latest, have to learn how we identify, understand and implement the values which are the basis of our social cohesion. Many migrants have strong religious identities because of the importance of religion in their cultures of origin. If they feel that their religious identities are at risk because of a clash with the values we see as basic to our social cohesion and because of the way those values are understood and lived out in Australian society, there is the potential for divisiveness and the loss of social cohesion which could put Australian society at risk. The challenge to Australians is to keep fine-tuning and adjusting the rules we follow in daily living to ensure that

Australia remains a fair and attractive society, a good society for all its people.

It is in this sense that Australians expect migrants to integrate into our secular multicultural democratic community. Nevertheless, that understanding of multiculturalism came under attack during the shock, anger and dismay many Australians felt following the New York and Bali bombings. Multiculturalism was blamed for a perceived reluctance of some members of our new migrant groups to become part of our society. Recent Muslim migrants were the focus of this concern.

Media reports from Europe on difficulties in integrating Muslim migrants, as well as graphic TV and press stories from the Middle East on suicide bombers, anti-Western violence, the treatment of women and the killings of critics and dissenters fuelled concerns across Australian society that Muslims might fail to integrate. As a result a minority began questioning the long-term possibility of multiculturalism and there was a resurgence of calls by some for a return to a policy of assimilation of migrants into the dominant Anglo-Celtic culture of Australian society.

Understandably, Muslims felt defensive in the face of such concerns. But, in fairness to the Australian host community, Muslim migrants need to remember that there is a deep-seated fear of Islam in the West linked to the 1400-year long historical experiences of Christians in the face of Islamic territorial aggression which continued into the 17th century. Nowadays, that fear is not so much about territorial aggression as about a perceived cultural aggression from Muslims within Western countries. There is a fear that Islamic influences in our society will put at risk some of the core values treasured in Western society – freedom of speech and of religion, equality before the law, democracy and universal human rights for both men and women.

A study into cultural diversity and religion published in 2004 found that twenty-five per cent of Australians thought that Muslims do not fit in. The same report noted that overseas conflicts:

> 'have put Australia's social harmony at serious risk, and secondly, that religious extremism has the potential to destroy the fabric of Australia's civil, pluralist and democratic society'. [1]

This uneasiness and the concerns which give rise to it are not confined to Australia. There is serious academic discussion and debate in both Western and Islamic societies about the compatibility of some Muslim religious beliefs and practices with the core values needed for the functioning of a democratic society.

Australian studies so far have highlighted the importance of access to jobs, education, health services and acceptance by the host community as factors which facilitate that 'wanting to belong' attitude among migrants which is crucial for integration and social harmony. But there has been little study of whether religion strengthens or undermines a migrant's desire to belong to and be part of the wider community. Unless migrants with strong religious identities find Australian core values to be good and no threat to their core religious beliefs, our social cohesion will collapse.

In pluralist societies like Australia the future will require a social cohesion built on an understanding of Australia as a community of various ethnic, religious and secular groups living and working together. That requires a shared understanding and acceptance of some key values and ways of respecting one another as well as a shared commitment to the wider community. It also requires an effort to clarify the role of religion in the public life of a secular democratic society.

2 THE RELATIONSHIP BETWEEN RELIGION AND POLITICS IN WESTERN SOCIETIES

Western societies find their roots deep in the religio-political history of the pre-Christian Middle East, as well as in the Greek and the Roman worlds. As people in the Middle East moved from a nomadic to a more settled way of life, leaders emerged who combined priestly and kingly functions in building their societies. As the king/priests became stronger and imperial ambitions grew, these kings or neo-emperors began to recognise the value of religion in unifying the diverse peoples of their expanding kingdoms. Acceptance of the king's gods and their worship became a foundation stone for the unity of the empire. These religious beliefs were able to tolerate the older, earlier gods, as long as the official gods of the empire were acknowledged and worshipped. But after the appearance of monotheism about 1500 BCE Judaism challenged that arrangement.

Their monotheism rejected the worship of the imperial deities which was the basis of unity and of citizenship within empires. Secondly, the Jews believed that kings, judges and the powerful were subject to God's laws. King David was admonished by the prophet Nathan because of his adultery with Bathsheba, and the killing of her husband - not for the Jews a king whose will decided what was right or wrong. They believed that a higher law limited the power of kings and governments. The influence of that insight is still with us in the limitations on the power of the state spelt out in the Constitutions of modern democratic societies.

Jesus Christ

The Jews, along with all peoples in pre-modern societies, made no distinction between politics and religion. To distinguish issues as political, social, economic and secular would have made no sense to them. All were religious issues, because they were subject to God's law. It was within this cultural setting that Jesus Christ appeared and began his teaching and challenge to the Judaism of his day.

The Jews of that period were looking for liberation from the oppression of the Roman Empire. Jesus argued that the true liberation of Israel from Rome and from its own oppressive authorities lay in persuading the people of Israel to repent and change their attitudes to others. For him, the centrality of relationships was crucial. The root cause of oppression, injustice and domination was to be found in a lack of compassion and the impact that had on the way society was structured. Jesus offered an alternative, the Kingdom of God.

This teaching had important political implications. In a society in which God's law and compassion were to be dominant, money, power, prestige and status would not be the principal values associated with the ruling authorities. They would use civil and religious authority to serve, not to dominate people. If the people of Israel continued to lack compassion, success in overthrowing the Romans would not make Israel any more liberated than before.

Jesus was calling people to that faith and trust in God which gives us hope and confidence that if we love our enemies, offer forgiveness to those who injure us, seek reconciliation and search for justice with compassion and a special care for the marginalised, then the beginnings of the Kingdom of God will already be in our midst.

The Kingdom of God will not be fully realised in this world because of human frailty, but

> 'To believe in God is to believe that in the end goodness and truth will triumph over evil and falsehood.'[2]

So firm was his conviction of this that Jesus refused to allow his disciples to use physical force to defend him from the authorities and execution. While Jesus offered no concrete political model for building a just and compassionate society, his relevance for modern societies lies in his insistence on compassion, justice and a refusal to use violence for religious purposes as the core of sound social, economic and political systems. His example was followed by his early disciples who suffered spasmodic persecution for the next 300 years but continued to attract others to share their faith.

Church and State in the Medieval period

By 313 CE, the Roman empire ended the persecution of Christians and granted freedom for all to practice the religion of their choice. Constantine moved his capital to Constantinople (Istanbul) and exercised his role according to the traditional Middle Eastern understanding of the priest/king role of an emperor. Eusebius of Caesarea summarised it as follows:

> 'one God, one Word and Saviour, one emperor whose role it is to interpret to the whole human race the knowledge and love of God.'[3]

The emperor Theodosius went the next step in 380 CE and declared Christianity the official religion of the empire. Monotheistic Christianity was now the state religion and had to clarify its relationship to the state.

In the East, the Byzantine church based in Constantinople found itself under the direct influence and control of Constantine and his successors. The Byzantine State was centred in the Sacred Palace and around the quasi-divine person of the Holy Emperor in Constantinople. There the Church found itself incorporated into a fixed social and political order which it failed to modify. It turned away from this world and focused its theology on the nature of the Godhead and adopted as its ascetical model the world-rejecting hermits of the desert. It tended to operate as an arm of the king or emperor seen as a semi-divine ruler with authority over both the political and religious life of the people. That relationship is still to be seen in countries which are part of the Orthodox tradition. As Huntington put it, '*In Orthodoxy, God is Caesar's junior partner; in Islam God is Caesar while for the Chinese and Japanese, Caesar is God.*'[4]

In the West, the Roman Church took a different course. It distinguished the Church and State, God and Caesar. Because of this, a different relationship developed and gave birth to what we know as Western Civilisation. The long struggle between the church and civil authority to set the boundaries between their respective authorities was an important element in that development.

From as early as the time of Constantine, Christian writers in the West were developing the implications of Jesus' distinction between a Christian's duties to religious authorities acting in the name of God, and their obligations to the civil authorities acting in the name of the emperor (Caesar). 'Render to Caesar the things that are Caesar's and to God the things that are God's' (Luke 20:25). They recognised that both Church and State received their authority from God, but clearly distinguished between the powers of the Church and of the State and resisted the interference of the state in religious matters. By the end of the 4th century, St Ambrose was arguing that:

> 'The Emperor… is within the Church, not above it, and consequently it is the duty of the Christian ruler to subordinate his action to the church's decrees in all matters that concern the faith.'[5]

And by 494 CE Pope Gelasius was acknowledging the authority of both pontiffs and kings but claiming greater responsibility for the pontiffs because of their spiritual role.

St Augustine also emphasised another important factor influencing the relationship between the spiritual and temporal. His pre-Christian Latin heritage – its concern with order, moral conduct and moral responsibility – were tools to be used in the Christian's struggle to create a new world.

This inspired the efforts of the papacy 'as represented above all by St Gregory, who laboured amidst the ruins of a dying civilisation to serve the cause of social justice and humanity'.[6]

Gregory the Great's contribution enabled the Church to engage with the new barbarian rulers and their peoples, setting the groundwork for the redevelopment of a new unity in Europe under Charlemagne some centuries later. The invasions by nomadic barbarian tribes such as the Huns, the Vandals and the Goths resulted in the collapse of the old Roman Empire in Western Europe and the loss of its classical Greek and Roman heritage. The Church stepped into the vacuum and took on the role of cultural leadership. It re-established educational institutions through its monastic schools which became the universities of Western society by the 12th century. Its courts remained for some time the only effective legal system left in the chaos of the empire's collapse, while its missionaries spread across Europe to seek the conversion of the tribes to Christianity. It provided an environment, a civil society which encouraged social and intellectual activity and the free and spontaneous transmission of ideas untrammelled by political control. This was the impetus behind the uniting of people of different races and language in shared cultural aims and in a fellowship of ideas and religious unity across Europe in Christendom.

Gradually a new political and religious culture began to develop, but one with its problems for the Church. The emergence of Charlemagne and the beginnings of the newly united Western Europe saw the increasing subordination of the Western church to the control of civil authorities. Charlemagne saw the Church as a department of state,

> 'which it was his duty to supervise and regulate along with other departments of life throughout his empire, a concept very similar to that held by emperors in the East'. [7]

His empire was basically a theocratic society whose leaders saw themselves as divinely appointed rulers and leaders of different peoples and languages held together by their common religious beliefs and bonds. A clash with the Catholic Church was inevitable.

In due course, things came to a head in the West with the election of Pope Gregory VII in the 11th century. Gregory VII was a reforming Pope who set out to liberate the church from political control. He initiated a

Papal Revolution in which the true making of the West and the expansion of Europe took place.

His purpose was crucial for the development of Western civilisation:

> ... the whole of Christendom, from its summit to its meanest village must be divided into two. One realm for the spiritual, one for the secular. No longer were kings to be permitted to poke their noses into the business of the church. [8]

Henry IV was emperor and attempted to force Pope Gregory to abdicate only to be forced by Gregory to come barefoot in the snow to seek forgiveness at Canossa in Northern Italy. Gregory also strove to end lay control over ecclesiastical appointments and to stop the buying and selling of church offices such as bishoprics. Eventually, the Concordat of Worms (1122 CE) came up with an agreement that the grants of land and property which went with the appointment of a bishop were the business of the state; the spiritualities, the selection and ordination of bishops, were to be the business of the Church.

Gregory also set in place legal structures and institutions for the Church which were adopted by the civil authorities and gave us the fundamental institutions of our Western legal systems. He went further. He also claimed supreme legislative and judicial power including the right to depose all princes and to have all Christians as his subjects.

But Western Europe didn't become a theocracy. A number of factors prevented such a development in spite of the apparent victory of the papacy over the civil powers. Essentially, the Church's spiritual authority was that of the Prophets of Israel, as recounted in the Old Testament of the Bible. These Prophets cajoled and criticised injustice and that self-interest which blinded rulers, judges and society to the plight of the poor, the widow and the orphan. That understanding of the Church's spiritual authority together with Christ's endorsement of the legitimacy of civil authority made theocratic claims contestable.

Secondly, the beginning of the centralisation of authority initiated by Gregory was expensive. The Vatican succumbed to the temptation to follow the example of the medieval states and use its rights of jurisdiction to raise money, with the inevitable abuse and exploitation of Catholics by Rome. It compromised the prophetic and evangelical stance of the friars, led to a growing anti-papal stance among reformers in the Late Middle Ages and lost credibility for the Church.

A loss of credibility also arose for the Church from the militaristic spirituality which began to influence Christianity during the barbarian invasions in the 5th and 6th centuries. This military spirituality was strengthened by Charlemagne's policy of demanding the conversion of defeated barbarian tribes in the 8th century. It peaked after Muslim attacks on Rome in the 9th and 10th centuries and during the Spanish struggle to take back control of its lands from its Muslim conquerors.

When Christian pilgrims were denied their traditional access to the Holy Land by new Muslim rulers, the popes unleashed that militaristic spirit by declaring crusades, first against the Muslims, secondly against heretics and sectarians in Southern France seen to be threatening religious unity and social cohesion.

The Crusades were a disaster. They failed as a long term solution to the access of Christians to the Holy Places, and 'stirred up a new aggressiveness against non-Christians, manifested at home in violent attacks on Jewish communities'.

They fatally weakened the ability of the Eastern Empire to defend itself against Islam; they permanently divided the Greek and Latin churches and militarised the sense of discipleship for laymen in the West. They also paved the way for the use of physical force and the Inquisition to counter heresy. Up until the 12th century the Church had resisted such measures.

Positive developments

Yet, all this can easily lead us to overlook significant developments at that time which were important steps in the overall development of Western societies.

First of all, there was a Renaissance. The emerging universities across Europe gained access to the Muslim libraries in Spain. Not only did this give philosophers and theologians access to many of the literary and philosophical works of ancient Greece and Rome lost with the collapse of the empire, but it also made available the great achievements of Islamic culture in mathematics, sciences and literature. These were major contributions to the beginnings of the Renaissance which peaked in the 15th century.

The acceptance by Catholic philosophers and theologians of that time of the validity of human reason in its own right was an important catalyst encouraging a critical and developmental approach to these new sources of knowledge. This openness to intellectual inquiry and, surprisingly, the work of artists were important: 'The art of the Renaissance was an art of observation and experiments, and it had a direct influence on the development of the study of anatomy and perspective.'

It was Leonardo da Vinci in the 15th century who first realised the possibilities of a science of experiment and applied knowledge which could give man mastery over nature.

Technological developments saw the harnessing of wind and water power and the introduction of printing. Parliaments were initiated, democratic city states began to be established, double-entry book-keeping in accountancy, and a re-interpretation of the ban on usury enabled banking systems to develop.

Secondly the power of the papacy was challenged from within its own ranks by churchmen during the 12th – 14th centuries influenced by developments of natural law thinking on the inherent dignity of the human person. Natural law presumes objective standards of behaviour and moral responsibility which limits the powers of those who exercise governance, both civil and religious. This leads at times to skirmishes between bishops and kings over the limits of their respective authorities and to protests over violations of the natural law. This is the creative tension which has fostered the freedom and the dynamic activity of Western culture.

Thirdly, the Franciscan spiritual revival which accompanied the social and intellectual renaissance in the 12th century fostered a growing awareness and respect for human dignity. The religious focus shifted from an emphasis on the majesty of Jesus, the ruler and judge, to his humanity. Francis of

Assisi built a close personal relationship with Jesus by bringing faith and daily life together with a deep concern for people and nature itself.

Fourthly, 'in the social movements of the 14th century,... for the first time the poorest and most oppressed elements of mediaeval society asserted their claims to justice.'[9] There was no fatalistic resignation to the pain and suffering of this life in the hope of salvation from it in the next life. Coming to terms with and seeking solutions to those problems in the here and now was important.

Fifthly, the paralysis of the Catholic leadership in the face of growing calls for reform of the Church created disillusionment and frustration. As the 14th century saw the beginning of the development of the nation state and the rise in nationalism the combination made a Reformation almost predictable.

These developments in pre-Reformation and pre-Enlightenment days were crucial to the development of modern Western society with its freedoms and rationality.

The Reformation

By the 16th century, the seeds of modernity sown in the previous centuries and a growing anti-papalism among Catholic reformers had begun to destabilise Western Europe. The unity of Christendom built on shared beliefs and values including the spiritual authority of the papacy fell apart in the 16th century.

At its beginning, Luther was not challenging the substance of the faith, but shifting Christianity from a church-centred to a Christo-centric, scripturally focused paradigm with 'a fundamental continuity of faith, rite and ethics'. But, he ended up revolting against the intellectualism of Aristotle and St Thomas and the whole Latin tradition. The Lutheran Reformation became 'a spiritual Peasant Revolt'. Its emphasis was on the freedom of Christians, the freeing of the believer from the doctrinal authority of the Pope and the freedom to interpret the Bible for oneself, appealing to the judgment of one's own conscience, and the further development of an ethic of personal responsibility.

Protestantism also rejected the contemplative ideal of monasticism and asceticism and substituted the standard of practical moral duty. It was essentially a religion of action. From this came its well-known characteristic – the Protestant Work Ethic.

Moreover, 'Faith was no longer a human participation in the Divine knowledge, but a purely non-rational experience – the conviction of personal salvation.' This is still a major feature of American Evangelical spirituality.

All these have become important factors in our understanding of responsibility and autonomy in the modern era.

The Enlightenment

After the Reformation, although Catholic and Protestant scientific thinkers shared ideas within an informal scientific community, at another level there was a sharper division between Catholic and Protestant which led to 100 years of religious wars and strife across Europe. These religious wars of the post-reformation period brought home to political thinkers not just in England but across Europe, the need for mutual tolerance if peace and order were to be re-established. The divisions which led to conflict were not only between Catholic and Protestant, but also within those denominations.

The Treaty of Westphalia in 1648 sought an end to the religious wars in Europe following the Reformation and made a beginning to the adoption of religious tolerance. Enlightenment thinkers such as John Locke and Montesquieu began to urge freedom of religion and the separation of Church and State. This was articulated in the American and French republican revolutions at the end of the 18th century, and adopted in the United Kingdom in the 19th century, ending official religious intolerance of Catholics in Britain.

Out of these developments came a number of important features of modern Western societies.

Democracy

Debates among Catholic theologians on the human rights of indigenous peoples in the newly discovered Americas and the Protestant emphasis on the dignity and the rights of the individual, nourished the seedlings of human rights and democracy planted during the Middle Ages. At the same time, the weakening of links to the papacy meant that kings were no longer subject to any oversight from the papacy nor to the accountability that went with that. The English Stuart kings soon saw themselves as sovereigns accountable only to God. The Protestants under Cromwell fought a civil war in the name of Parliament against the claims of the Stuart kings and notions of religious freedom, at least for Protestant Dissenters, began to be accepted in England. In 1680 the English Revolution introduced the concept of a constitutional monarch, an important development for democratic political systems. That growth was furthered by the declarations on human rights made by the American and French Revolutionaries.

Radical Secularism

The scientific discoveries of the age were part of a development of ideas about life and society which had its roots in the Catholic belief in the power of reason to unlock the laws of nature. At the same time, the religious conflict over the Reformation fuelled a deep hostility towards the Catholic Church because of its power and perceived wealth. It was particularly 18th century intellectuals who accused the Church of enslaving the minds of people during the Middle Ages and of being anti-science.

The criticism of the Church for its stance on Galileo has been one of the key arguments used to sustain this accusation. Strangely, while Galileo was under attack, it was Jesuit contemporaries of his who named mountains on the moon and developed the mathematical methods to provide us with our Western calendar still in use after 400 years. Recent research claims that it was Galileo's failure to use scientific evidence in his premature attacks on scripture which led to his condemnation by Rome.[10] Painting Catholicism as being anti-science suited the agendas of powerful forces as an anti-clerical, non-Church Deism gave birth to an open atheism or agnosticism and a radical secularism.

Radical secularism rejects faith and the supernatural in favour of reason. It sees no need for that belief in a God creator whose existence and plan for mankind provided the frame of meaning for pre-modern peoples; it opposes any role for religion in public life and confines it to the private life of the individual. These views are often linked to a strong belief in the potential of scientific method to unravel all the mysteries of life and their impact has undermined the credibility of religion for many people. This critique ignores history, including the history of science, and is based on beliefs that are open to the same charge of irrationality as that used about religion - they too operate on the unprovable assumption that science can unravel the mystery of life.

Those attitudes are now under pressure. Atheistic secular ideologies have been associated with major atrocities under Lenin and Stalin, Adolf Hitler, Mao Zedong and the Khmer Rouge. It is not only religion which can be ambivalent about violence. This is also evidence that radical atheism has difficulty in protecting human rights. Jurgen Habermas has acknowledged that and has called for a coalition of secularists and religious people to meet that need.

It would be mistaken however to assume that all forms of secularism are by definition anti-religious. It may be true of French secularism which has had such an influence in the Islamic world, but it is not true in most Western secular societies. At the other end of the continuum from doctrinaire secularist states are those democratic societies which insist on a separation of Church and State but are not officially hostile to religion. Western civilisation is therefore a complex mixture of different components – 'secularism, the state, society, church and religion.... [its] dominant tenor, including that of the state, includes religiosity, a characteristic clearly observed in the Anglo-Saxon part of the Western world.'[11] Australia is a good example.

3 RELIGION AND POLITICS IN ISLAMIC SOCIETIES

Muslim migrants in Australia come largely from Islamic societies where the relationship between religion and politics appears to be quite different from that in Australia and in other Western democracies. They also bring an awareness of close but difficult relationships with Western Europe and Christendom over 1400 years. In the past, those difficulties related largely to disputes over territory: some during the Islamic empire's expansion; some during the Crusades and others during Ottoman advances to the gates of Vienna in the 17th century, and Western colonial domination during the 19th and 20th centuries. Currently, Palestine, Iraq, Afghanistan and Iran are reminders that such difficulties continue, and some of the interventions by the West are seen by many Muslims as a threat to Islam. Any critical comments on Islam by someone writing from a Western and Christian perspective are open to criticism as prejudiced, misinformed and polemical. But, if made in good faith, they may well signal potential difficulties for maintaining social cohesion in a multi-faith society. The issue of social cohesion in pluralist societies is so important that there is a professional responsibility: 'not to submit to voluntary censorship, but to deal with these matters fairly, honestly, without apologetics, without polemic, and of course, competently'.[12]

Islam:Muhammad

Muhammad appeared in the 7th century CE at a time of social turmoil and ferment in Arabia, where polytheism and tribal anarchy still prevailed. He sought a solution to the blood vendettas and warfare as well as to the collapsing traditional family and social values being undermined by affluence in the trading city of Mecca. He announced that, under divine guidance, he had received a solution to the spiritual and socio-economic concerns of the Arab tribes. He would challenge the 'unbridled materialism, avarice, and corruption which he saw as a condition of ignorance and unbelief, and would unite the tribes into a confederation with shared goals and a single faith'.[13]

That faith had to be something new and universal. His spiritual experiences inspired him to seek acceptance of monotheism and the formation of a super-tribal community of belief as the cement to unite Arabia. His inspiration came during his regular practice of retreat and prayer on the mountainside outside Mecca. From about 610 CE he began to undergo a series of spiritual experiences in which he claimed that God spoke directly to him through the Archangel Gabriel who dictated God's message. These experiences over the next 20 years until his death in 632 CE resulted in the compilation of the Qur'an which Muhammad and his followers believed to be God's word revealing his law and plan for mankind. It was these experiences and Muhammad's understanding that he was called to be the messenger of God, that was the source of his spiritual and political vision.

The beliefs of Islam are not complex – that all are called to submit to the One God, to take personal responsibility for their life and actions and, as members of the religious community, to build a society in which justice, compassion and peace will reign. That demands that God's law be adopted and obeyed. Muhammad's role:

> was to provide an eschatalogical vision, knowledge of God's will, right guidance and social leadership. He worked to create a community based on shared religious beliefs, ceremonies, ethics and laws – transcending traditional structures based on families, clans and tribes.[14]

He sought to win all Arabs to membership of the Islamic community. This involved not just an individual's acceptance of faith in the one God, but of membership of a community of believers whose way of life and its political, economic and social institutions are regulated by the law of God as revealed in the words of the Qur'an and in the Prophet's explanations and applications (the Sunna). This 'meant that all the actions of the individual and all the instititutions of the state should express a fundamental submission to God's will'. In this way, Islam would establish God's rule on earth by building the community into an Islamic state, the House of Islam. This is the basic rationale for Muslim political and moral activism.

The Prophet Muhammad had a socio-cultural background drawing on Judaism, Eastern Christianity and 3000 years of Middle Eastern civilisation. In those cultures, the political, cultural and religious leaderships were all merged in the civil power. It was these institutional patterns which Muhammad adopted for Islam.

After a very slow and difficult start for his mission because of persecution in Mecca, Muhammad became convinced that he would have to hold a more prominent and powerful position if his mission were to bear fruit. 'People would not be moved by ideas alone, but only by ideas propounded with commanding prestige.'

He took his followers away from the hostile community in Mecca to Medina where his success as an arbitrator and military leader saw him become the principal leader of a community of nine clans. There he drew up a Constitution which recognised the identity and rights of both the Islamic community (the Umma), and those of the non-Muslim Jewish tribes of that town. In that first Islamic state:

> The constitution of Medina established a pluralistic state – a community of communities. It promised equal security to all and all were equal in the eyes of the law.[15]

Muhammad built his political power on the Arabian tribal tradition in which weaker groups entered into pacts and treaties with stronger tribes for protection against enemies. Muhammad used his personal charisma as well as his growing spiritual, military and political standing to offer alliances to tribes. This guaranteed mutual protection and peace for the members of the network and protection for Islam from non-Muslim enemies. By doing this, Muhammad built up a strong network of tribes in alliance with him throughout Arabia, giving him extraordinary authority and leverage in controlling the Islamic state. As his power grew, he required conversion to Islam as part of any pact with a tribe, thereby building a federation of tribes, an Islamic state linked by religious affiliation throughout the whole of Arabia.

By seeking and obtaining political power Muhammad sought to achieve one of Islam's central goals:

> to provide a stable, just and peaceful society in which Muslims can practice their faith... [but] the rules governing that society must be correctly drawn from the Qur'an and the sunna.[16]

Its purpose was to protect the religious freedom of Muslims and allow them to earn a livelihood for themselves and their families as members of the Islamic community.

It also established a set of rituals and practices known as the Five Pillars:

1. Muslims witness in prayer and everyday life to the oneness of God and to Muhammad as his Prophet: 'I bear witness that there is no god but God and that Muhammad is the Messenger of God.'.
2. Muslims are expected to offer five daily prayers at dawn, noon, afternoon, evening and night.
3. Muslims pay a social tax to be shared with the poor.
4. Muslims fast during the month of Ramadan.
5. Every Muslim who can afford it goes on pilgrimage to Mecca at least once in a lifetime.

In this way, Islam became a community-state, both a faith and a political order seeking to transform the world through action in the world. It is 'the universal mission of the Muslim community to spread God's rule and law through teaching, preaching and, where necessary, armed struggle.'[17]

Clearly, Muhammad was a religious and political visionary. He integrated military power (jihad) into the work of his mission and used it and political power to enshrine and enforce Islamic law in society. This resulted in the members of the Islamic community seeing themselves as a chosen people with a mission to convert or conquer the world and thereby establish God's rule on earth. That rule has come to be expressed in Islamic societies as the Shari'a.

The Shari'a

The word 'Shari'a' brings to mind for many Australians, overseas press reports of women being flogged for immodesty, thieves having hands amputated in punishment for their crimes and women being stoned to death for being caught in adultery. While it is true that such measures of the Shari'a are still carried out in areas under the control of the Taliban and other radical fundamentalist regimes, those harsh penalties from the seventh and eighth centuries Arabia were introduced at a time when there were no courts, police or gaols. Strict rules of evidence made it quite difficult to impose these penalties and were intended to ensure that the number of cases were few. Their main purpose was to make an example of a few cases in order to encourage conformity to the law. Over the centuries as other options became available, the use of such penalties declined to the stage that they are now largely the monopoly of radical, fundamentalist extremist regimes. These regimes claim to be implementing the Law of God, the Shari'a. But mainstream Muslims see the Shari'a, not as a list of harsh penalties to be imposed for improper behaviour, but as a set of guidelines or rules which will enable Muslims to engage with daily life in an Islamic way. They seek guidance through the Shari'a just as Christians look to Jesus and the Gospels for guidance in building their relations with one another and in establishing a just and peaceful society.

The Shari'a is a common law system based on the writings of the Qur'an and the reports about the Sunna – the explanations and practical guidance which the Prophet Muhammad gave to his early disciples on how to travel on the correct path to God. These reports on the Sunna were compiled into anthologies called the Hadith. The Qur'an and the Hadith were the sources used by Religious Scholars to provide guidance to the faithful on how they should live their lives in submission to the One God. The foundation of it all is the Qur'an.

The Qur'an

The Qur'an is the very foundation of Islam. Muslims believe it is the very word of God dictated to Muhammad by the Archangel Gabriel. Its historicity as a collection of the teachings of Muhammad is not in serious doubt, but because of its style, it is not easy to follow. It isn't a history of Muhammad's life but more an insight into his thinking and his understanding of God's advice and guidance for him. This lack of historical context makes it difficult to fully understand the debates and to identify the opponents opposing him and his teaching. There is also a lack of detailed direction in the Qur'an on how a Muslim should live his or her daily life. Consequently there is need for guidance.

The Hadith and the Religious Scholars/Jurists

The Caliphs as the successors to the Prophet should have provided that guidance but their authority began to erode very quickly. The demands and temptations of empire were a factor. In pre-modern societies the only effective form of government was that of an absolute monarch with all the risks that arise from the lack of accountability, the authoritarianism inevitable in such a form of governance and the temptation of a luxurious courtly life-style. Empire pushed the Caliphs into that kind of role, but with a loss of credibility as religious leaders. Instead, the need for guidance in daily life led to the emergence of Religious Scholars or Jurists who gained credibility as informed and reputable moral and religious guides for the faithful. They looked to the Qur'an and the traditions associated with the sayings and example of Muhammad and his associates for guidance on how to live in the correct way. The Scholars or Jurists provided clear legal rules to enable Muslims to make a reality of their mission to build 'a just society that surrendered wholly and in every detail to God's will'[18]

Groupings of Religious Scholars (the Schools of Law) gradually emerged These were given a measure of recognition by the Abbasid Caliphs. As the latter had the power to appoint the judges, they appointed as judges only men with legal scholarship acceptable to the schools. In return, the Abbasids pressured the legal schools to get some degree of uniformity in their rulings and decisions. Scholars were also required to give reasons for their views. The pressure resulted in all Sunni jurists gradually accepting that if there were no explicit Qur'anic ruling, then a decision should be based on the teachings in the Hadith. This resulted in a degree of uniformity, with the schools fully accepting each other's rules and practices.

In the search for guidance, jurists also drew on customary practice as well as on the use of analogy and consensus to determine proper Muslim behaviour and religious life. Gradually they came to be seen as the real guardians of the heritage of the Prophet taking over the religious leadership role from the Caliph. As the legitimacy of the Caliph or Sultan's rule depended on his observance of the rules of the Shari'a or Islamic law, to ignore or violate that law was to put his dynasty at risk of losing its legitimacy in the eyes of the Religious Scholars and therefore in the eyes of the Muslim community. The Religious Scholars became a counter-balancing power base within Islam which limited the power of the Caliph or Sultan.

The Caliphs did attempt to get some uniformity from the different schools of law by appointing Religious Scholars as judges and controlling their decision making, but the Religious Scholars defended themselves against dismissal by avoiding new interpretations of the law. They appealed instead to precedents in the opinions and actions of the earlier scholars. In the meantime, a growing fragmentation of the Caliph's political role saw the rise of local leaders who took power in distant provinces of the empire. These sultans tended to concentrate on the temporal, secular dimension of their roles, thereby strengthening the religious leadership of the jurists.

This near total transfer of religious leadership to the Religious Scholars led to a form of separation of the functions of the political and religious leadership within Islamic societies. In effect, the Religious Scholars had the ability to insist that the ruler, the Caliph or Sultan, must remain within the bounds of the Shari'a or risk being stripped of his legitimacy. In the Ottoman Empire for example,

> 'As the price of this legitimation, the Scholars insisted upon some measure of executive limitation. Islamic law was in principle the law of the empire – and that meant the Sultan was subject to the law, not above it...Sultans earned the caliphate at the price of accepting that God and his law were above them.'[19]

The Religious Scholars took responsibility for interpreting and developing Islamic Law (the Shari'a), while the Caliph or Sultans maintained responsibility for matters of state. The Sultan was still expected to exercise some level of religious leadership by ensuring that the institutions of society complied with the Shari'a (Islamic Law) because classical Islamic political theory saw the faith as the regulator of life and society. The temporal ruler's function was to carry out religion's decrees.

The Caliphs, Muhammad's successors should have played a major role in the religious leadership of the community, but they kept losing authority with both Sunni and Shia Muslims. The Sunni are those who believe that the Caliph should be elected by the consensus of the Islamic community. The Shia insist that he should be a member of the Prophet's family.

In the case of the Sunni, there was a long debate and struggle within Islam over the created or uncreated quality of the Qur'an, over whether it could be subject to rational reinterpretation. Black points out that it was only in the tenth and eleventh centuries that the uncreated character of the Qur'an was finally accepted. It was a defeat for the Caliphate which had backed those supporting the created character of the Qur'an, but a victory for the *ulama*. The Caliphate finally lost 'authority'; it was left only with power. It was the Qur'an and the Sunna as interpreted by the Religious Scholars which had authority. The Religious Scholars had gradually become the acknowledged interpreters of the word of God and the religious and moral leaders of the community. The Scholars began to limit the use of reason in the process of interpretation by proclaiming that the Qur'an was uncreated and that it was their role to interpret it and guide the community because they had the special knowledge needed for this role:

> [This] deprived the Caliph of any say in the definition of Islamic norms [so that] justice was defined independently of the political rulers or state authority. What was happening was that religious, social and economic legislation was being enacted from below.[20]

In this way Islam became a political community based on law and ritual rather than on political institutions. It also left the Caliphate without authority and politically weakened so that there was a partial split between the religio-moral-legal authority which belonged to the Scholars and the politico-military power left to the Caliph.

The victory of the Religious Scholars came at a price. Patronage had given the Caliphs a degree of power over them. As the various Schools of Law emerged the Caliphs began appointing judges from the ranks of those Religious Scholars/jurists who had been trained in those schools. There were risks for the scholars in this if their decisions angered the ruler. To avoid the risk of losing their positions because of unpopular decisions, some sought to rely on precedence to justify decisions and reduce the ruler's influence. Interpretation (*Ijtihad*) and independent judgment were both casualties. Consequently, literal-fundamentalist tendencies were strengthened by arguing that the Qur'an could not be re-interpreted because of its uncreated character.

Although the Sunni mainstream saw the consensus of the community, expressed through Religious Scholars, as the source of Islamic law, the arrival of the Mongol invaders disempowered the community as the source of consensus. The Mongols did not want the Shari'a becoming a subversive code. They encouraged its development into 'a system of established rules, which could not jeopardise the more dynamic dynastic law of the ruling house'. This resulted in the democratic consensus of the community as a guide to God's law being reduced to the consensus of the Religious Scholars. Their opinions had become so authoritative that many argued that further re-interpretation was considered no longer necessary and the gates of interpretation were closed. But, as Feldman argues, the Shari'a is very like our Common Law system which evolves through the use of precedent, common sense, reason and analogy and this process has continued within Islamic communities. Nevertheless, the use of precedents, the widespread acceptance of the Qur'an as the uncreated Word of God and the use of the Hadith for guidance has resulted in a narrowing of the framework within which Muslim Religious Scholars seek direction. The use of reason has been under pressure.

In contrast to the Sunni tradition, the Shi'i Muslim groups developed their own system of guidance on law and moral precepts which looked to a direct descendant of the Prophet to guide them. They looked for that from the fourth Caliph who was a member of Muhammad's family, but was assassinated in 661 CE. He became the first Imam of the Shi'a community; it was to him and to the succeeding group of Imams, the Twelve, that the main group of the Shi'as looked for guidance on the Qur'an. The sixth Shi'i Imam, Jafar As-Sadiq developed a school of law known as the Jafari school which tended to play down consensus as the source of guidance and looked for guidance from the teaching of the Imams who were regarded as infallible.

When the eleventh Imam died in 874 CE while under house arrest imposed by the Caliph, his young son who was to be his successor could not be found. The 'agent' used by the Imam under house arrest to communicate with the Shi'a community eventually announced that the twelfth Imam had gone into hiding. This doctrine of the Occultation of the Hidden Imam led the Shi'a to accept the leader of the Religious Scholars as the representative of the Hidden Imam.

God provides each generation of Muslims with an Imam, who as the rightful leader of the community is imbued with...a sovereignty which comprises both religious and, at least in theory, political authority...In the eyes of their followers, the Shi'i Imams retained that role as authoritative interpreters of divine law.[21] The first 12 Imams were considered infallible and the Shi'a look to them and to the members of the household of the Prophet for guidance while they await the return of the Hidden Imam.

In the light of these comments on Sunni and Shi'a efforts to continue reinterpreting the sources of Islamic Law, claims that the gates of *itjihad* or re-interpretation have been closed in Islam since the twelfth and thirteenth centuries are an over-simplification. There is certainly a strong tendency among Muslims to interpret the contents of the Qur'an and the Hadith literally and use this as the guide to the correct path. But, as already noted above, the Shari'a has always been accompanied by an acceptance of those local laws and customs which do not clash with it. The Shari'a continues to evolve and adjust to the context in which people find themselves. Claims that Islam is essentially incompatible with democracy can certainly be challenged and are being challenged by a growing number of Muslim thinkers.

The Expansion of Islam

Within 100 years of the death of Muhammad, Islam controlled an empire which included areas which had been major centres of Christian belief. Jerusalem first of all, then Syria, Egypt, Iraq and Iran, Roman Africa, Spain and parts of southern France fell to the Muslim armies. Most have gradually converted to Islam over the centuries. While Islam did use military force (jihad) to expand its empire, it didn't force conversion on the conquered. But the territorial conquests of peoples did facilitate Islam in 'imposing its own social and political order on them and then looking for conversions, which were not slow in coming'.[22]

Conversion to Islam was attractive for some members of conquered groups because of their lack of prospects as second class members of an Islamic society. They also resented the extra tax burden imposed on them as non-Muslims. Others were attracted by the spirituality and simplicity of Islam, but many continued to maintain their traditional non-Muslim faiths for many centuries. In recognition of and acceptance of this reality,

Islam adopted a form of governance developed in the Sasanian (Persian) empire. Non-Muslim groups who were considered to be 'peoples of the book' and who accepted an alliance with their Islamic overlords were given a degree of autonomy and self-rule under Islamic authority. Nevertheless, minorities within Islam didn't achieve that equality under the law implied in the Constitution of Medina, as some modern Muslim interpreters claim. In fact minorities are still finding such equality difficult to achieve in Islamic states.

Islam, the Islamic state and history

Underlying all this is a Muslim mindset which experiences the presence of God in the historical trials and tribulations of political life and state affairs because Islam has sacralised public life. Muslims accept that there is an inherent structure and correct social shape for this world and believe that by following the essential rules which they have understood through the Qur'an and Islamic law, they can guide history to its triumphant fulfillment.

Unlike Christianity which is 'a religion of triumph out of adversity, of salvation in the midst of defeat', Islam is 'a religion of triumph in success, of salvation through victory and achievement and power.' [23]

The spread of Islam as far as Southern France in the west to the border areas of China in the east and as far as sub-Saharan Africa in the south was seen as a sign of God's power and confirmation of the validity of Islam and the role of the Islamic community as God's chosen people. It was inevitable then that the collapse of the Islamic empire with the conquest of Baghdad by the Mongols in 1250 CE marked the first great crisis in Islamic history.

Islam came up with various constructive responses. Religiously it turned very much towards Sufism, a mystical interpretation of Islam which existed mainly among an elite during the classical Arab period. Non-Arab Islam is now steeped in Sufism; and even Arabian Islam has been deeply influenced by it. Sufis were more focused on the individual and the eternal rather than society and the historical. They were inclined to stress God's love rather than his power and emphasised internal renewal rather than correct behaviour and conformity to Islamic Law.

This spirituality was a strength in the face of adversity, but it never became the official version of Islam, and in spite of its major role in the spread of Islam through India and South East Asia, is still regarded by many Muslims as almost heretical.

Secondly the Mongols who initially sought to overthrow Islam became Muslim and a new flowering of Islamic power and culture took place in Persian and Turkish areas. By the 16th century the Ottoman (Turkish) empire was at its peak and Islam had doubled its geographic expansion, spreading into the Balkans, deeper into Africa, the sub-continent and as far as the southern Philippines in the east. Yet, Muslims have never given this medieval period the same recognition they give to the classical period.

But its triumph was short-lived. By the 18th century it was in serious decline. There was the disintegration of military and political power at a time when the West was growing in power and influence and much of the Islamic world was being colonised by Western powers. This perceived defeat was another major crisis for Islam. Something had gone wrong and a search began for solutions which would reinvigorate Islamic society so that it would 'once again flourish as a divinely guided society should and must'. [24]

The first assessment of what had gone wrong led to protests against the causes of the deterioration of Islamic society and spirituality. One of the earliest and still influential protests was that of Ibn 'Abd al-Wahhab (1703-1787). He and his followers rejected corruption, laxity and the affluence of the medieval empire. They also rejected the mystical way of the Sufis and any dissensions such at that of the Shias over the selection criteria for a Caliph. They insisted solely on the strictest, puritanical, vigorous and literal implementation of the guidance of the Qur'an and sunnah, not in an ideal form, but as it was originally implemented in the 7th century.

Another influential reformer was Shah Waliyullah of Delhi (1703-1781), a Sufi, who rejected corrupted forms of Sufism, and any tolerance of a decadent society. He stood against internal decay and external threats of domination while accepting Islamic development. He was more flexible than the Wahhabis and willing to renew within the existing structures. But he insisted that Muslims must not accept the contemporary decline. His political ambition was to restore Muslim power in India on the Mughal model. Pure Islam must be re-enacted; a regenerated Muslim society must again be mighty. His ideas were developed by his followers into a stand against colonial domination.

In the 19th Century Jamalu-d-Din Afghani (1839-97) became the catalyst focusing attention on what should unite all Muslims regardless of divisions – a nostalgia for the departed earthly glory of pristine Islam and a stand against the colonial imperialism of a powerful West. He inspired political revolutions and encouraged the development of reason and technology in order to be strong again. He lifted Islam out of a widespread passivity and fatalism into that dynamic, exuberant ferment of the present day. He was part of a movement triggered by contact with the West during the early stages of modern colonialism. That contact highlighted for many Muslims the contrast between conditions in Europe and the decline of Islam throughout the Muslim world. They blamed despotism as one of the key causes of Islamic decline, and began discussing democracy as a possible solution.

The autocracy of the absolute rulers in Islamic history was an old problem. Although autocracy 'was fundamentally opposed to the spirit of the Qur'an',[25] the Religious Scholars either avoided making an issue of it or were unable to mount an effective challenge to this violation of the Shari'a. The actions of rulers in funding the building and maintenance of madrasas and the appointments of Religious Scholars to paid posts as judges certainly meant that there was a conflict of interest for the Religious Scholars. They were part of the problem. The consensus of the community, the people, had been reduced to the consensus of the Religious Scholars, an unaccountable and elite group. The democratic spirit of early Islam was lost and autocratic rule and despotism flourished.

Later in the 19th century and into the 20th an Islamic liberalism appeared, particularly among Muslims who had been educated or influenced by the West. However, the values of liberalism were never integrated with the religious faith of Islam. A person could be both a Muslim and a Westernised liberal by ignoring the basic conflicts involved. Liberalism's political outcomes were adopted, but not the premises on which those conclusions were based. Its appearance was short-lived but influential for a time among the liberal leaders of Muslim societies.

After the First World War, the carve up of the Ottoman Empire among the victorious allies of that war – France, Britain and Italy, and then the abolition of the Caliphate by the secular government in Turkey, shifted political thinking from the problem of despotism to the struggle against colonialism and to the hope of restoring some kind of Islamic unity. During this period, Hasan Al-Banna (1904-1949), an Egyptian, founded the Muslim Brotherhood.

Al-Banna set as goals for his organisation the liberation of the Islamic homeland from colonial domination and the establishment in its place of an Islamic state faithful to Islam precepts, social regulation and its mission to all of mankind. This was the Muslim Brotherhood's response to the collapse of the Caliphate. They saw the awakening and mobilisation of the Muslim community, the umma, as the way to re-establish Islamic governance. They were confident that the West would collapse because of its immorality, usury and political divisions.

After the Second World War, following the collapse of colonial control, Westernised elites moved into power and set up single party regimes or absolute monarchies. In the name of modernisation they attempted to secularise their countries. Egypt under Nassir took strong action against the Brotherhood. The challenge within Islam now changed again, this time it was to defend the cultural identity of the Islamic community, the umma.

In a number of Muslim countries, the introduction of secularism was not a good experience. Modernising leaders followed the French, almost Jacobin version of Doctrinaire or Radical Secularism. As a consequence, there has been a back-lash in the Islamic world, not just against colonialism but also against the desacralising of their societies. Countries like Turkey, Egypt, Morocco, Algeria and Iraq have experienced heavy handed anti-religious treatment and this, together with a deep resentment of continuing Western neo-colonialism, has resulted in a still growing fundamentalist back-lash. Even some progressive Muslim thinkers are calling for modernisation without secularisation. They see secularisation as a rejection of God, as self-centred individualism and as the promotion of promiscuous sexual behaviour and mindless consumerism.

From the time of the suppression of the Muslim brotherhood in 1950 until the 70s, the writings of Sayyid Qutb (1906-66) and of Mawdudi (1903 – 79) were influential. Qutb drew on Mawdudi's theory that Islam had reverted to a state of *jahiliyya*, decadent and ignorant. This means that true Muslims will also be in conflict with those within Islam itself who are really 'apostates'. Qutb rejected democracy but Mawdudi did not. He believed that Islam was democratic because of the tradition of *shura* (consensus) and that by engaging in elections it would be possible to hand authority to the righteous.

Said Hawwa, a Syrian disciple of Qutb's noted that when Muslims are a majority democracy is no threat.to them. It was his more positive attitude to democracy which has led to the gradual abandonment in recent years of violent confrontation and the adoption of the democratic path by a number of Islamist factions. Hezbollah in Lebanon and Hamas in Palestine seem to be going down this track. But democracy may not be the real goal. Hawwa saw democracy as a means to the implementation of Islam. Where does that leave non-Muslims in an Islamic state?

A different approach has developed in what is called the Maghreb school of thought. These thinkers, led by Malik Bennabi (1905-73) saw the advent of European contact as a chance for Islam to break out of its decadence, not so much by blaming the despotism of leaders but by acknowledging the lack of critical thinking and a kind of moral paralysis afflicting Muslim society. He saw democracy demanding attitudes and sentiments towards one-self and the other, as well as the provision of socio-political conditions which are necessary for those sentiments to develop in a community. For him, this requires an education process which leads to the development of a democratic sentiment in the consciousness of people, Rachid Ghannouchi and other thinkers of this school have gradually influenced Islamic movements to shift their position on democracy:

> Islam has come back to restore dignity to its followers, to liberate them from despotism, to regain the Ummah's usurped legitimacy, to restrict the powers of the state, and to establish and reinforce the power of the people, the power of civil society...[26]

The Gulen movement in Turkey is also attempting to revitalise Islam. It has a commitment to *ijtihad* (re-interpretation) which has led it to offer leadership in education in the humanities and science as well as in an openness to 'others' which makes dialogue constructive and may lead to a more positive Islamic engagement with the modern world. However, there are a number of responses other than the democratic. They need to be seen in the context of Islam's overall response to its decline: the use of nationalism, apologetics and fervent dynamism.

Islamic nationalism draws on both Western and non-Muslim Asian nationalisms. It seeks freedom from 'infidel' domination, a desire it shares with other strands of nationalism. But in the case of Islamic nationalism, the more it has reached out to the masses, the more and more religiously inspired it has become. Because Islam gives 'spiritual significance to the group, and strengthens the human tendency to stress a closed society and to identify it with a religious one this has contributed to its failure to adopt the positive side of nationalism, the sharing of rights and welfare with all members of the nation.'[27] Nation for a Muslim means 'the Islamic community'. [28]

Apologetics refers to those writings and media programs which seek to defend Islam against attacks, disbelief, modernity and Westernisation Its main purpose is to keep more liberal Muslims committed to Islam by showing them and reassuring them that Islam is still sound. They do this by insisting that there are no problems – that Islam is compassionate, just and merciful, that women are completely free within Islam, that minorities have equal rights and that Shari'a Law is an adequate formula for a just and compassionate society. But when one asks what is Shari'a law, one finds that there is no consensus. The difficulties encountered in countries like Pakistan and Malaysia in developing Islamic Law to meet the challenges of being part of pluralist, democratic societies are a serious problem for apologists. Their apologetic approach has 'diverted the attention of contemporary Islamic thinkers from their central task – the central task of all thinkers to pursue truth and to solve problems'.[29]

They leave that to revelation. Revelation offers principles. Reason and experience have to be used to find practical solutions to the problems encountered in any society.

Dynamism refers to the calls for greater activity among Muslims to stir them out of passivity and fatalism. Unfortunately these calls have all too often been made without any setting of limits or boundaries. This has resulted in a lot of activity ending up in the violence of a mob full of zeal to defend Islam and to recover its former glory, but lacking a coherent program to achieve a just and compassionate society. This is fuelled by a fundamentalism which has rejected many of the underlying assumptions and values of modernity. They have gone back to the roots of Islamic faith and practice to find in the Qur'an and the Sunna the formula, the Shari'a for an Islamic state. So far the challenges of gender, minorities and violence have eluded them.

Other fundamentalists, better described as radical Islamists see 'holy war' (jihad) and violence as necessary tools for this work. They see non-Muslims and Muslims who disagree with them as 'infidels' and have shown little compunction in using terrorist massacres to achieve their aims. When they do succeed as the Taliban did in Afghanistan, they set up a state based on a harsh Wahhabist interpretation of the Shari'a.

This more radical Islamist response is exemplified in the thinking and practice of Al-Qaeda and the Taliban in using military jihad. By doing this they seek to gain political control as its means of defending Islamic societies from Western influence and to bring down Muslim governments which are seen to be allies of the West. Even Muslim majority countries with a tradition of tolerance and democracy like Indonesia have found the influence of this group difficult to subdue. Close allies of the USA like Britain and Australia have discovered that there is even some support for radical Islamism among its own Muslim citizens.

These radical Islamists put pressure on those Muslims who urge the acceptance of religious freedom and tolerance, who seek changes in the status of women, and call for some degree of separation of Church and state in Islamic democracies. The Islamists confront the more open thinking of people like al-Ghanouchi. The result has been a struggle for the soul of Islam, still under way in this 21st century. It is a struggle which essentially revolves around the relationship between religion, politics, human rights and the use of coercive power to force observance of what are believed to be the laws of God and therefore Islamic Law.

These difficulties give rise to concerns which have to be faced in countries such as ours. Australia is a signatory to the United Nations' Universal Declaration of Human Rights, but 56 Islamic countries, as members of the Organisation of Islamic Conference, have given only qualified support to that charter. Their alternative Cairo Declaration on Human Rights insists that the freedoms and rights must be in accordance with the Islamic Law (Shari'ah). This has caused difficulties over divorce in India, conversions from Islam to Christianity in Malaysia, and continuing discrimination against minorities in Muslim countries. Underlying this 'are traditional interpretations of Shari'a that support principles like male guardianship of women (*qawama*), sovereignty of Muslims over non-Muslims (*dhimma*), and violently aggressive jihad.'[30]

These are issues that Muslim Australians will have to address as part of what Abdullah Saeed calls their contract with Australian society.

4 RELIGION AND POLITICS IN THE AUSTRALIAN SECULAR STATE

❖

In Islamic societies religion is very much part of public life. Daily calls to prayer, public celebrations of Ramadan, an official role for Religious Scholars in giving legal advice on personal, family and heritage law as well as on issues of religious law and its enforcement, all give religion a public role no longer possible in secular, democratic societies. Catholicism too played such public roles in feudal, pre-industrial societies, but in secular democratic societies, both Islam and Christianity are being challenged to find new ways of playing that public role without undermining the principle of the separation of church and state.

In the past, many of the basic values on which societies, Christian and Muslim built their social cohesion were religious beliefs, and acceptance of those beliefs was the basis of full citizenship. Minority beliefs and believers tended to be marginalised.

We have to find an alternative. While it is true that Muslim-ruled areas were an early form of multi-faith and multi-cultural societies, the use or adoption of their models of governance as a form of multiculturalism in today's democracies will not work unless ways are found to ensure the equality of all before the law. Working through the challenges that all religions face today will be no easy task as Catholicism has found in its long and continuing struggle to come to terms with such a society . Secularists too are challenged. They are having to face up to the reality of religion even in this post-modern era and to the possibility that a religious basis for our values may provide as firm, if not firmer foundation than do atheistic or utilitarian ideologies. This final section considers those challenges.

Challenges for Radical Secularists

The radical secularist critique outlined above is that religion is irrational, hostile to science, a source of violence and conflict, opposed to free speech and a threat to the separation of Church and State. It ignores the fact that rationality is much wider than scientific evidentialism.

> We 'know', not only when we are presented with publicly observable evidence, but also, crucially, through experience ... Experience is often not publicly accessible, repeatable, readily or fully describable, predictable, objective, amenable to experimetal control and measurement, or capable of expression in the form of general laws.'[31]

Yet scientists use it all the time in developing their hypotheses. But if scientific hypotheses are given the status of facts, this is bad science. Religion does not necessarily oppose science but challenges that narrow reductive materialism which is itself a belief system. Secularists need to address this challenge and recognise the narrowness of the definition of rationality in their thinking.

The religious challenge to Australia's secular democracy

Legally, the Australian state is not hostile to religion. Under its Constitution

> The Commonwealth shall not make any law for establishing any religion, or for imposing any religious observance, or for prohibiting the free exercise of any religion, and no religious test shall be required as a qualification for any office or public trust under the Commonwealth.[32]

Ours is a form of secularism which requires the government to protect the freedom of religion and the freedom of speech of its citizens but without preferencing one religion or belief system over the others. It avoids the inequalities which inevitably arise from basing citizenship on religious affiliation. The state also has a responsibility to intervene if religious activities violate the freedoms and rights of others or become a threat to public safety and the common good. These are important elements of what is known in Australia as the separation of Church (organised religion) and State.

Once the separation of Church and State was adopted in western societies, citizenship and loyalty to the state could no longer be based on a single religious identity for all citizens. A new foundation for social harmony and cohesion had to be found which included religious freedom and the religious tolerance implied in that.

For religious believers religion has a crucial, on-going role in public life, particularly in contributing to the maintenance and strengthening of the values on which Australia builds its social cohesion. Pope Benedict XVI argues that to ignore the role of Christianity in the development of Western civilisation is to cut off that civilisation from its spiritual and moral roots. Without such nourishment, it will wither and die.

To do this, Christians and Muslims urge us to build society on the laws of God and to reject those secular views which want religion confined to the private sphere. The question though is how to do that in a secular democracy.

Historically, the Churches in Australia have played an important role in public life – in pioneering and providing community development, educational, health and welfare services for communities and acting from time to time as a public advocate for the disadvantaged. This was, and still is, an important source of nourishment for those basic values and institutions on which we build our social cohesion as a society. However, there are pressures in society which are reducing that potential of religious groups. Some come from the radical secularism of the media and sections of academia..

The pressures of contemporary culture keep religion impotent in the public sphere. The message is that 'it is perfectly all right to believe that stuff' provided you keep it to yourself; in other words, the only form of religion permitted becomes a 'trivialisation of faith', something on the level of a hobby, but 'not really a fit activity for intelligent, public spirited adults.'[33]

In spite of this disdain for religion, there are still significant levels of religious and spiritual belief in the Australian community. Formal membership of religions may have decreased, but positive attitudes towards religion and its contribution to public life are still alive here. This is something radical secularists cannot ignore. They have to allow a place for religion within the public life of the community while, rightly, resisting any attempt by religious groups to use the state to preference them in some way either financially or by enforcing their religious beliefs and practices on their own members or on the community generally.

This implies that some of the barriers experienced by religious groups such as Christians and Muslims arise from unresolved problems within their own groups. As both Christians and Muslims believe that their missions involve transforming society, their religious leaders have to resist the temptation to reclaim traditional roles in society and 'try to take over society as a whole and make one's counter-modern religion obligatory for all…'[34] Such an approach is ultimately a failure to accept the implications of religious freedom and to face the reality that many Australians no longer have any religious affiliation. As many as 16% of Australians seek meaning and fulfillment through non-religious belief systems. They too have to be part of the search for those shared values needed as a basis for our social cohesion.

There is also the reality of the self-inflicted wounds which have damaged the public credibility, particularly of Catholicism and of Islam. The paedophilia scandals and the mistreatment of children in Catholic children's homes have been quite damaging and the perceived ambivalence of some sections of Islam towards violence have tarnished Islam's status for many. Unless both religions are seen to be more positive in tackling the root causes of these issues, their lack of credibility will continue to undermine their capacity to nourish Australian society and culture.

There is also the lingering damage caused by the leadership of the Catholic Church in the 19th century, particularly because of its reaction to the treatment it received from the French Revolution. It found it difficult to accept liberty, equality and fraternity, French style. It rejected freedom of speech, freedom of religion, the separation of Church and State and democracy itself. Catholics in English-speaking countries including Australia were less negative, and in fact participated fully in political and public life. They saw little threat to Catholicism in these values and as minorities, fully availed themselves of them. The American John Courtney Murray's reflections and theologising on that experience contributed to a major change in attitude from the leadership of the Catholic Church in the 1960s at Vatican II.

The Second Vatican Council accepted that freedom of religion is essential for human dignity. The Catholic Church now accepts the separation of Church and State and its implication that citizenship can no longer be based on religious belief, but it still continues to claim the right and responsibility to challenge the State in the event of serious violations of justice and basic human rights This is not inconsistent with the Australian constitution and our tradition of freedom of speech.

Islam in Australia may well go down the same path. There are already indications that Muslim Australians, like earlier Catholic migrants, are generally comfortable with the religious freedom, freedom of speech, democracy and the kind of secularism we have in this country. However, in spite of all that, influential sections of both Catholicism and Islam in Australia are struggling with the relationship

The challenge for Islam

Islam today is experiencing a fundamental spiritual crisis as it attempts to come to terms with the challenges posed by the multi-faith, multicultural societies which globalisation has made inevitable. Islam has shown a capacity in the past to overcome such crises, but this one is posing a challenge which is much more difficult because it requires a reinterpretation of the Qur'an and the Sunna for a 21st century context. This is not impossible. The Qur'an provides Muslims with a basic constitution for mankind and is untouchable, 'but the by-laws under it may be renewed and reviewed'.[35] In other words, there is a flexibility in interpreting the application of the Qur'an in particular circumstances. In the past, many Muslims:

> 'could see meaning in the Quran that went far beyond the literal sense of the words, and which transcended the circumstances of the original revelations. The Quran became a force in their lives that gave them intimations of the sacred, and which enabled them to build fresh spiritualities of great power and insight.'[36]

Some of the traditional interpretations of Islamic Law regarding military jihad, Muslim superiority over non-Muslims under the system of restricted citizenship (*dhimmitude*) and the male guardianship of women all need re-interpretation in multicultural and multi-faith democracies. There are other important challenges. Within Islam in Australia there are occasional calls for the recognition of aspects of Islamic Law and reservations expressed about the separation of church and state.

Shari'a Law does present a number of difficulties because of its differences with Australian law. Its regulations cover a range of personal, family and commercial areas which are part of the legal system in most Muslim countries. In Australia, some of those provisions clash with Australian law – there is a limited right to polygamy; there are some inheritance and divorce regulations which do not treat women equally with men; there are regulations on marriage which discriminate against women and non-Muslim partners. There are also positives of course. There is growing interest in Islamic banking for example, which may have valuable insights for Australian financing.

Over the centuries the Sharia law, drawn from the guidance of Religious Scholars, developed and evolved to meet changing situations and challenges. It was built on the Qur'an and Sunna but also drew on local traditional practices and precedents. In many ways it was like English common law, built on precedent, but constantly embracing new insights and solutions to problems of injustice.

In reality the biggest hurdle for Islam in secular democracies like Australia will be having to relinquish the right to have Islamic law recognised and enforced by the State. Such a recognition is contrary to our understanding of the separation of Church and State but that distinction is not accepted by influential Islamic scholars who believe it separates religion from political life. Experience of life in Australia's secular democracy may lead Islamic thinkers to realise that there are other ways of contributing to public life without having to recognise the majority religion as the state religion. Over the centuries Islamic Law, the Shari'a, has evolved to adjust to local situations and cultural realities which are not seen as a threat to its core beliefs and there is no reason to think that such developments won't take place in Australia. Such thinking is surfacing among Muslim scholars in the USA.

Even if Shari'a law is not adopted in Australia, that does not prevent Muslims from observing it as a private decision. Catholics also have a Code of Canon Law covering the discipline to be followed by Catholics. The fact that the State doesn't recognise it still leaves Catholics free to follow it in their own lives. It shouldn't be a real problem for Muslims in Australia, apart for the few who may wish to exercise as a Muslim, the restricted right to polygamy, presuming of course that some of the traditional interpretations are rethought for democratic political situations.

There is also the reservation among Muslims about the sovereignty of the people as the source of authority in secular democracies. Islam insists that only God is sovereign, not the people. However, as the sovereignty of the people is more concerned with the accountability of the legislative, judicial and executive arms of government, it does not rule out the Sovereignty of God. There is an implicit recognition of that sovereignty in limits to the power of the state as set out in the Constitutions of democracies. Religious believers would see in this a recognition of the sovereignty of God.

The challenges for Catholics

Catholics also have their problems. There is confusion within Catholicism over the roles of bishops and Catholic politicians in public life. This is seen in their well-publicised clashes from time to time on issues such as abortion and stem-cell legislation.

Conservative Catholic Bishops in recent US Presidential elections threatened Presidential candidate, the Catholic John Kerry with refusal of the Eucharist because of his stance on abortion; some bishops spoke out against Barak Obama during the recent campaign because of his policy of limiting, not banning abortion. Conservative Catholics in the United Kingdom protested against former Prime Minister Tony Blair's reception into the Catholic Church because of his vote in favour of allowing abortions up to 24 weeks of pregnancy; Cardinal Pell in Sydney threatened Catholic politicians with exclusion from the Eucharist if they should vote to expand stem-cell research in that state.

The post-election row when Notre Dame University invited President Obama to speak at the university highlights the seriousness of this confusion. Even though Pope Benedict XVI recently set out principles on which this confusion could be resolved, little has changed:

> 'This political task is not the immediate competence of the Church. Respect for a healthy secularity – including the pluralism of political opinions – is essential in the Christian tradition... Only by remaining independent can she... form consciences, ... be the advocate of justice and truth, [and] educate in individual and political virtues: that is the fundamental vocation of the Church in this area.'[37]

The pope is telling his Bishops that they do not have any authority as bishops to decide on the best methods to be used to achieve political goals. That is the responsibility of the civil authority. The church's task is to offer guidance on the morality of our behaviour, conscientise its members, and through them, society generally, on the principles and basic values needed for 'building a society worthy of man'.

The political task is the responsibility of the politicians. The Pope doesn't spell out the nature of that responsibility but Catholic tradition has always distinguished between religious and civil authority, that of God and that of Caesar. It was the opinion of St. Thomas Aquinas that the primary concern of the civil authority is social order and the common good. Not everything immoral should be criminalised.

Acceptance of that view is implicit in the Vatican's Declaration on Procured Abortion:

> 'The law is not obliged to sanction everything, but it cannot act contrary to a law which is deeper and more majestic than any human law: the natural law engraved in men's hearts by the Creator…'[38]

The Vatican statement concedes that the law is not obliged to criminalise everything that is immoral, but it does remind politicians and voters that we cannot ignore the possibility that certain actions amount to being an intolerable evil and must be criminalised. The genocidal Holocaust is an undisputed example of this. The politician has no alternative but to criminalise such behaviour. But what must the Catholic politician do when a society is deeply divided over the morality of an issue like abortion? A commentator on St Augustine claims that he saw good reason not to criminalise behaviour which does not have strong community support:

> Laws, he felt, will not be respected or enforced unless they enjoy at least the assent, if not the active support, of a critical mass of the community (which, he considered, a ban on prostitution would not). It is damaging to society and to the rule of law to make laws which are not going to be respected or enforced. Therefore they should not be made. [39]

This means that a politician, even if personally convinced that abortion is morally wrong, is called to make a judgment on whether criminalising abortion will better serve the common good than legalising or tolerating its use in a range of circumstances. The politician is called to make a prudential judgment as to whether criminalising or decriminalising immoral behaviour is in the interests of public order, the enhancement of human dignity and the common good .[40]

A Catholic politician who accepts the judgment of a bishop that a certain behavior is immoral, may still make an informed conscientious decision that criminalising such behavior may cause serious difficulties for social cohesion in a society and damage the common good. A Catholic politician with an informed conscience is one who draws not just on revelation but also on reason, research and experience in reaching a decision.

The Church as institution does not have the authority to override the God-given right and obligation of the politician to follow his informed conscience in making such practical judgments on the legislation before parliament. Tony Blair's vote for abortion up to 24 weeks can be supported by Catholic theology as a responsible, morally justifiable, prudential judgment to minimise harm being caused by objectively immoral actions. In fairness to politicians, bishops should be mindful of what both Aquinas and Augustine had to say about the practical judgments of politicians before condemning their decisions.

The search for practical political solutions to achieve a fair and just society is the direct responsibility of civil society. If religion is to continue to influence public life religious leaders should focus on assisting their members to grow into a mature faith and the fullness of their humanity. Believers as citizens share in the search for a just society. But, they too, when voting as citizens are making a prudential judgment on what is likely to be the best outcome in the circumstances. Normally, except in extraordinary circumstances, church and mosque leaders should not play a role in marshalling votes on party political issues.

Their role as religious leaders in public life is to assist in the development of the conscience of society, thereby being 'critical collaborators' in seeking the common good. If religious leaders gave greater priority to enhancing the acceptance and observance within their own groups of those key universal and Australian values which are the basis of our social cohesion – human rights, equality before the law, gender equality, freedom of speech and freedom to change one's beliefs, the credibility and influence of religion would be enhanced.

When the Catholic Church engages in the public arena, it is useless and unfair to non-Catholics simply to claim a special guidance from God on whether to criminalise a particular action. The Church must commit itself to using civic reasoning to win support for any concerns it may be raising about immoral behavior. Quality and convincing argumentation will only come if there is freedom among Catholics to debate crucial questions related to issues such as abortion, stem-cell research, euthanasia and gay marriages. That is not happening at present. Catholic newspapers act as if all these questions have been decided by the Pope using his infallible teaching authority. This censorship of ideas reduces the Church's ability to engage in effective public debate.

And there is more. The Church's credibility in the public square has been damaged by the paedophile priest problem and the sexual abuse of children in institutions. In these cases, the lack of proper avenues of appeal within the Church when administrative decisions failed to investigate or to provide mediation for people, reinforces the hostility and rejection of religion as a potential contributor to the maintenance of the values at the basis of our social cohesion. The Catholic Church cannot ignore the challenges of lifting censorship on debate and developing procedures which ensure accountability for administrative decisions.

The church cannot form virtuous men and women for public life if crucial moral questions are off limits for discussion within the Church. The use of 'creeping infallibility' to reduce debate ends up emphasising that blind obedience which gives us people in public life who have an Eichmann mentality – that of one who just follows orders.

Having said all that, issues such as whether Pope Pius XII should have been more direct in challenging the Nazi policies towards the Jews, shows that even Popes have to make difficult practical judgments on what to do when confronted by immoral actions. There is no doubt that he saw the Holocaust as grossly immoral. His dilemma was whether public condemnation might cause even worse horrors for people under Nazi control. He can be criticised for the effectiveness of his practical judgment, but hardly accused of voting for the Holocaust. Bishops should keep that in mind when criticising politicians who refuse to criminalise immoral actions

The responsibility of religious leaders is to form communities of people committed to living according to the spirit and the example of Christ or Muhammad, both in their own personal lives as members of religious communities, and in their public lives as citizens. It is the role of believers as citizens to actually work out politically how to build a society of justice, compassion and concern for the common good. There is no definitive template given by Jesus, Muhammad or other religious founder as the solution. Finding solutions is our task as citizens, and religious believers support as wide a range of political solutions as there are political parties in this country. Hopefully those solutions will bring greater respect for truth, justice, equality and the common good. But we are human. We don't always get it right as experience teaches us if we are willing to learn from it.

Catholicism is still working its way out of the confusion it is experiencing in playing a role in public life which does not violate the principle of the separation of Church and State. Islam in Australia will have to go through a similar experience. It cannot avoid the challenges and the inevitability of being challenged on some of its assumptions about the role of religious law in public life.

The challenges for both Christianity and Islam

Both Christianity and Islam have to face up to the implications of their attitude to others. Missionary religions can fuel an exclusivist mentality which sees 'others' as alienated from God, or the enemies of God and a threat to 'true believers'. Catholic theology of mission has been grappling with this question since the Second Vatican Council in the 1960s and the concept of 'mission' is being developed in a much more inclusivist way. This has led to the Catholic Church participating more positively in ecumenical and inter-faith activities. Mission is still announcing the Gospel but with more emphasis on respect for and learning from the spiritual insights of other religious denominations and traditions, and on building bridges and alliances which urge their members to tackle together poverty, injustice, environmental challenges and social conditions which are destructive of human dignity. Crucial to this Prophetic Dialogue is the acknowledgement of the presence of God's Spirit at work in peoples of other religious traditions and of non-religious belief systems who demonstrate love and compassion for others especially in their work to overcome poverty and injustice for those outside their own families and communities in the wider society.

Islam from its beginnings acknowledged the action of God within Judaism and Christianity. As it spread and encountered other major religions, it sought to acknowledge them also as religions of the book. This more tolerant, inclusive type of Islam is under threat today because of the exclusivist Wahabbi attitude to 'others' being popularised throughout the Islamic world. Australia will best counter this tendency by maintaining and strengthening Inter-faith dialogue, not just between mainstream Christian denominations, Islam, Buddhism, Hinduism and Sikhism, but together with the more evangelical and fundamentalist streams of Christianity which are still very uncomfortable with such dialogue.

Finally all belief systems must find some degree of agreement on human rights particularly freedom of religion, and gender equality. In doing this, religious groups will use revelation as a guideline in seeking solutions, but when seeking to influence public opinion in a multi-faith society, they must use the tools of civic reasoning, drawing on evidence from research and experience in seeking to influence public opinion in a multi-faith democracy. Inter-faith and multicultural dialogue has to search for an agreed understanding and acceptance of universal human rights. It has to do that and do that in the spirit of reciprocity, equality and mutuality if social harmony is to be maintained.

CONCLUSION

There is need for secularists and religious believers to work towards consensus about the meaning of the separation of Church and State in Australia. Dreams of turning Australia into a radical secularist state on the one hand or a Confessional State, be it Christian, Islamic, Buddhist or Jewish on the other, have to be challenged. Such dreams are incompatible with fundamental universal and Australian values such as equality under the law, freedom of religion, and freedom of speech. At the same time there is a need to acknowledge that religion has had and still has a role in public life, especially in contributing to the clarification and nourishing of the key principles and values which should be the basis of our social cohesion. That clarification will have to involve dialogue on the role of reason and an acceptance of the need for evidence from research and experience supporting religious views. Believers must sell their solutions using the persuasiveness of civic reasoning. If that path is taken in interfaith and civic-multicultural dialogue, the encounter of Catholicism and Islam with Australian secular society will be constructive for us all.

Endnotes

[1] Desmond Cahill et al., *Religion, Cultural Diversity and Safeguarding Australia*, Canberra, Department of Immigration and Multicultural and Indigenous Affairs, and Australian Multicultural Foundation in association with the World Conference of Religions for Peace, RMIT University and Monash University, 2004, p.8.

[2] Desmond Cahill et al., *Religion, Cultural Diversity and Safeguarding Australia*, Canberra, Department of Immigration and Multicultural and Indigenous Affairs, and Australian Multicultural Foundation in association with the World Conference of Religions for Peace, RMIT University and Monash University, 2004, p.8.

[3] Albert Nolan, *Jesus Before Christianity, The Gospel of Liberation*, London, Darton Longman and Todd Ltd, 1977, pp.83-85.

[4] Hastings, Adrian (ed.) '150-550' in *A World History of Christianity*, Grand Rapids and Cambridge UK, William B Eerdmans Publishing Company, 1999, p.38.

[5] Huntingon, Samuel P, *The Clash of Civilizations and the Remaking of the World Order*, New York, Simon and Schuster,1996, pp. 69-73.

[6] Dawson, Christopher, *Progress and Religion*, New York, Image Books, 1960, p.130.

[7] Dawson,1960, p.134.

[8] Ward, Benedicta & Evans, G.R, 'The Medieval West', in Hastings,1999 p. 115.

[9] Holland,Tom, *Millennium: The End of the World and the Forging of Christendom*, London, Little, Brown 2008, p. xviii.

[10] Dawson, 1960, p. 138.

[11] Woods Jr.,Thomas E, *How the Catholic Church Built Western Civilization*, Washington, Regnery Publishing, Inc., 2005, pp. 69-74.

[12] Glasner,P.E., *The Sociology of Secularisation: a critique of a concept*, London, Routledge, Kegan Paul, 1977 p. 140.

[13] Lewis, Bernard *Islam and the West* ,Oxford:1993, quoted in Warraq,

Ibn (ed.), *The Quest for the Historical Muhammad*, New York, Prometheus Books, 2000, p. 9.

[14] Esposito, John L, *Unholy War: Terror in the Name of Islam*, Oxford, Oxford University Press, 2002, p.30.

[15] Lapidus, Ira M, *A History of Islamic Societies*, Cambridge, Cambridge University Press, 1988, p.34.

[16] Khan, MA Muqtedar, 'Ijtihad: A Return to Enlightenment' *The Compact of Medina: a Constitutional Theory of the Islamic state*. Published in the *Mirror* international 30 May 2001. Available from http://www.ijtihad. org/compact.htm; Internet; accessed 13 October 2004.

[17] Clark, Charles, *Islam (Religions of the World)*, San Diego, Lucent Books Inc, 2002, p. 30; The Sunna refers to the Hadith – the collected stories about the life and teaching of Muhammad – and customary practices, p.106.

[18] Esposito, John L, *Islam, the Straight Path*, 3rd Edition, New York & Oxford, Oxford University Press, 1998, pp.34-35.

[19] Armstrong, 2000, p. 41.

[20] Feldman, Noah, *The Fall and Rise of the Islamic State*, Princeton and Oxford: Princeton University Press, 2008, p.54.

[21] Crone & Hinds, *God's Caliph: Religious Authority in the First Centuries of Islam*, Cambridge University Press, 1986, quoted by Anthony Black, *The History of Islamic Political Thought: From the Prophet to the Present*, Edinburgh University Press, 2001, p.33.

[22] Berkey, 2003, pp.131-132; 138-139.

[23] Jacques, Jomier, *How to Understand Islam*, London, SCM Press Ltd, 1989, p.1.

[24] Cantwell Smith, Wilfred *Islam in Modern History*, New Jersey: Princeton University Press, 1957, p.31.

[25] Cantwell Smith, 1957, p.41.

[26] Armstrong, Karen, *Islam: A Short History*, London, Weidenfeld and Nicolson, 2000, p.98.

[27] This is a quotation from Rachid Ghannouchi, cited in Tamimi, Azzam, *Rachid Ghannouchi: A Democrat Within Islamism*, New York, Oxford University Press, 2001, p.179.

[28] Cantwell Smith, 1957, p.80.

[29] Cantwell Smith, 1957, p.77.

[30] Cantwell Smith, 1957, p.87.

[31] An-Naim, Abdullah 'Shari'a and the State' in Islam and the Islamic State:

Negotiating the Future of Shari'a, Harvard University Press, 2008 in website edition, at http://sharia.law.emory.edu/en/book/export/html/17 sect. 1, 1.

[32] Furbey, Robert, 'Controversies of 'public faith', in *Faith in the Public Realm: Controversies, policies and practices*, Adam Dinham, Robert Furbey & Vivien Lowndes (eds.), Bristol, The Policy Press, 2009, p. 23.

[33] *Australian Constitution*, Sect. 116.

[34] Gallagher, Michael Paul *Clashing Symbols: An introduction to Faith and Culture*, London, Darton, Longman & Todd, 1997, p. 4, summarising the argument of Stephen Carter, *The Culture of Disbelief*, New York, Basic Books, 1993; Armstrong, Karen, *The Spiral Staircase*, London, Harper Perennial, 2005, p.137, and Maddox, Marion *God Under Howard: The Rise of the Religious Right in Australian Politics*, (Sydney Allen & Unwin, 2005,p.237, describe similar attitudes.

[35] Peter L Berger, 'Secularism in Retreat', in *Islam and Secularism in the Middle East*, Azzam Tamimi and John L Esposito (eds.), London, Hurst & Company, 2000 p. 40. '[To] 'try to take over society as a whole and make one's counter-modern religion obligatory for everyone – a difficult enterprise in most countries in the contemporary world... unlikely to succeed. And this unlikelihood does have to do with modernisation, which brings about very heterogeneous societies and a quantum leap in intercultural communication, two factors favouring pluralism and not favouring the establishment (or re-establishment) of religious monopolies.'

[36] Cragg, 1973, pp.186-187.

[37] Armstrong, 2000, p.65.

[38] Pope Benedict XVI Address to the *Inaugural Session Of The Fifth General Conference Of The Bishops Of Latin America And The Caribbean*, 13 May 2007. http://www.vatican.va/holy_father/benedict_xvi/speeches/2007/may/documents/hf_ben-xvi_spe_20070513_conference-aparecida_en.

[39] Sacred Congregation For The Doctrine Of The Faith, *Declaration On Procured Abortion*, Rome, 18 Nov 1974 S.21, at http://www.vatican.va/roman_curia/congregations/cfaith/documents/rc_con_cfaith_doc_19741118_declaration-abortion_en.html , accessed 21 April 2009.

[40] See the series of articles by 'Peregrinus' on Christian Morality in the online magazine *Catholica Australia* at http://www.catholica.com.au/peregrinus/044_pere_160507.php, accessed 11 Dec. 2007.

Bibliography

'Australia Deliberates: Muslims and Non-Muslims in Australia: Final Report', *Issues Deliberation Australia/America,* 4 March 2007. Ch 6 provides a summary, conclusions and recommendations, at http://ida.org.au/content.php?p=dpprelease accessed 26 Feb 2008.

Al Naim, Abdullah 'Shari'a and the State' in Islam and the Islamic State: Negotiating the Future of Shari'a, Harvard University Press, 2008 in website edition, at http://sharia.law.emory.edu/en/book/export/html/17

Alberigo, Giuseppe & Kononchak, Joseph, *History of Vatican II, Vol. V,* New York, Orbis Books, 1995.

Al-Ghannouchi, Rachid. 'Secularism in the Arab Maghreb.' In *Islam and Secularism in the MIddle East,* edited by Azzam Tamimi and John L. Esposito, London, Hurst & Company, 2000.

Ali, Tariq *The Clash of Fundamentalisms: Crusades, Jihads and Modernity,* London; New York, Verso, 2003.

Aly, Waleed, *People Like Us: How arrogance is dividing Islam and the West,* Sydney, Picador Pan MacMillan, 2007.

Armstrong, Karen, *Islam: A Short History,* London, Weidenfeld and Nicolson, 2000.

Armstrong, Karen, *The Spiral Staircase,* London, Harper Perennial, 2005.

Bat Ye'or in *The Myth of Islamic Tolerance: How Islamic Law Treats Non-Muslims,* Robert Spencer (ed.), New York, Prometheus Books, 2005.

Berkey, Jonathan P, *The Formation of Islam: Religion and Society in the Near East, 600 – 1800,* Cambridge, Cambridge University Press, 2003.

Berman, Harold J, *Law and Revolution: The Formation of the Western Legal Tradition,* Cambridge Mass., Harvard University Press, 1983.

Bevans, Stephen B and Schroeder, Roger P (eds.), *Constants in Context, A Theology of Mission for Today,* New York, Orbis Books, 2004.

Black, Antony, *The History of Islamic Political Thought: From the Prophet to the Present.* Edinburgh University Press, 2001.

Bosch, David J, *The Transforming Mission: Paradigm Shifts in Theology of Mission,* New York, Orbis Books, 1991.

Brennan, Frank, 'Respect For Politicians Who Represent All Of Us Is Crucial', *Eureka Street,* 12 Sept 2007, http://www.eurekastreet.com.au/article.aspx?aeid=3027 accessed 1 November 2007.

Burleigh, Michael, *Earthly Powers: The Clash of Religion and Politics in Europe, from the French Revolution to the Great War,* New York, Harper Collins, 2005.

Burleigh, Michael, *Sacred Causes: Religion and Politics from the European Dictators to Al Qaeda,* London, Harper Perennial, 2006.

Cahill, Desmond et al., *Religion, Cultural Diversity and Safeguarding Australia,* Canberra, Department of Immigration and Multicultural and Indigenous Affairs, and Australian Multicultural Foundation in association with the World Conference of Religions for Peace, RMIT University and Monash University, 2004.

Cantwell Smith, Wilfred, *Islam in Modern History,* New Jersey: Princeton University Press, 1957.

Clark, Charles, *Islam (Religions of the World),* San Diego, Lucent Books Inc, 2002.

Collins, Paul, *Between The Rock and a Hard Place: Being Catholic Today,* Sydney: ABC Books, 2004.

Cragg, Kenneth, *The Mind of the Qur'an,* London, Allen & Unwin Ltd, 1973.

Crone & Hinds, *God's Caliph: Religious Authority in the First Centuries of Islam*, Cambridge University Press, 1986.

Crone, Patricia, 'What do we actually know about Mohammed?', in www.openDemocracy.net, 31 August 2006.

Dawson, Christopher, *Religion and the Rise of Western Culture*, New York, Image Books, 1958.

Dawson, Christopher, *Progress and Religion*, New York, Image Books, 1960.

'Declaration on the Relationship of the Church to Non-Christian Religions' in *The Documents of Vatican II*, New York, America Press, 1966.

Dinham, Adam, Furbey, Robert and Lowndes, Vivien, *Faith in the Public Realm: Controversies, policies and practices*, Bristol, The Policy Press, 2009.

Duncan, Bruce, *Crusade or Conspiracy? Catholics and the Anti-Communist Struggle in Australia*, Sydney, UNSW Press, 2001.

Edwards, Benjamin, *Wasps, Tykes and Ecumaniacs: Aspects of Australian Sectarianism 1945 –1981*, Melbourne, Acorn Press, 2008.

Esposito, John L, *Unholy War: Terror in the Name of Islam*, Oxford, Oxford University Press, 2002.

Esposito, John L, 'Islam and Secularism in the Twenty-First Century' in *Islam and Secularism in the Middle East*, Azzam Tamimi and John L Esposito (eds.), London, Hurst & Company, 2000.

Esposito, John L, *Islam, the Straight Path*, 3rd Edition, New York & Oxford, Oxford University Press, 1998.

Feldman, Noah, *The Fall and Rise of the Islamic State*, Princeton and Oxford: Princeton University Press, 2008.

Gallagher, Michael Paul, *Clashing Symbols: An introduction to Faith and Culture*, London, Darton, Longman & Todd, 1997.

Glasner, PE, *The Sociology of Secularisation: a critique of a concept*, London, Routledge, Kegan Paul, 1977.

Haeri, Fadhlalla, 'The Jafari Schjool of Shari'a' in *The Elements Of Islam, 1990*, at http://www.mb-soft.com/believe/txw/jafari.htm

Hastings, Adrian (ed.), '150-550' in *A World History of Christianity*, Grand Rapids and Cambridge UK, William B Eerdmans Publishing Company, 1999.

Herbert, David, *Religion and Civil Society: Rethinking Public Religion in the Contemporary World,*, Aldershot: Ashgate Publishing Ltd, 2003.

Holland, Tom, *Millennium: The End of the World and the Forging of Christendom*, London, Little, Brown 2008.

Hughes, Philip, *Putting Life Together: Findings from Australian Youth Spirituality Research*, Fairfield,, Fairfield Press/Christian Research Association, 2007.

Huntingon, Samuel P, *The Clash of Civilizations and the Remaking of the World Order*, New York, Simon and Schuster, 1996.

Hurley, Jennifer A (ed), *Islam: Opposing Viewpoints*, San Diego, Greenhaven Press, 2001.

Inglis, Tom, *Moral Monopoly: the Rise and Fall of the Catholic Church in Modern Ireland*, 2nd ed. Dublin, University College Dublin Press, 1998.

Jensen, DM, 'Faith and Politics: The Rhetoric of Church-State Separation', in *Australian Religion Studies Review*, Vol. 18, No.1, 2005.

Jornier, Jacques, *How to Understand Islam*, London, SCM Press Ltd, 1989.

Khan, MA Muqtedar, 'Ijtihad: A Return to Enlightenment' in *The Compact of Medina: a Constitutional Theory of the Islamic State*. Published in the *Mirror* international 30 May 2001. Available from http://www.ijtihad.org/compact.htm; Internet; accessed 13 October 2004.

Kirby, Michael, 'Fundamental Human Rights And Religious Apostasy', The Griffith Lecture 2007, Queensland Conservatorium, Griffith University, 16 November, 2007, accessed 23 Jan 2009, http://webdiary.com.au/cms/?q=node/2185/print&PHPSESSID=c0ac7cfb28414fcbf8cbec91b25afa1b

Kung, Hans, *The Catholic Church*, John Bowden (trans.) London, Phoenix Press, 2002.

Lakeland, Paul, *The Liberation of the Laity, In Search of an Accountable Church*, London & New York, Continuum, 2003.

Lapidus, Ira, M, *A History of Islamic Societies*, Cambridge, Cambridge University Press, 1988.

Lewis, Bernard, *Islam and the West*, Oxford,1993.

Linden, Ian, *Global Catholicism: Diversity and Change since Vatican II*, London, Hurst, 2009.

Macgregor, Duncan et al., *Imagining Australia: Ideas for our Future*, Crows Nest NSW, Allen & Unwin, 2004.

MacQueen, Benjamin, Baxter, Kylie and Barlow, Rebecca (eds.), *Islam and the Question of Reform: Critical Voices from Muslim Communities*, Melbourne University Press, 2008.

Maddox, Marion, *God Under Howard: The Rise of the Religious Right in Australian Politics*, Sydney, Allen & Unwin, 2005.

McBrien, Richard, *Catholicism* (2 vols), Melbourne, Dove Communications, 1980.

McGrath, Alister, *The Twilight of Atheism: The Rise and Fall of Disbelief in the Modern World*, New York & Sydney, Galilee - Doubleday, 2006.

Madigan, Daniel, 'A Common Word Between Us and You: Some initial reflections.' *Thinking Faith* 18 January 2008, pp.1-3, at <http://www.thinkingfaith.org/articles/20080118_9.htm> accessed 22 January 2008.

Minnerath, Archbishop Roland, *Caesar's Coin: How Should Church And State Interact?* in Australian E-journal of Theology, 11, Easter 2008 at http://www.acu.edu.au/acu_national/schools/theology/ejournal/aejt_11/caesars_coin

Nolan, Albert, *Jesus Before Christianity, The Gospel of Liberation*, London, Darton Longman and Todd Ltd, 1977.

Peregrinus, 'The Morality of Cruising', in *Catholica Australia*, http://www.catholica.com.au/peregrinus1/079_pere_260308.php accessed 11 Dec. 2008.

Pontifical Council for Justice and Peace, *Compendium of the Social Doctrine of the Church*, Washington, United States Bishops' Conference, 2005.

Pope Benedict XVI Address to the Inaugural Session of The Fifth General Conference of The Bishops of Latin America and The Caribbean, 13 May 2007. http://www.vatican.va/holy_father/benedict_xvi/speeches/2007/may/documen ts/hf_ben-xvi_spe_20070513_conference-aparecida_en.

Ratzinger, Cardinal, 'Europe's Crisis of Culture', 1 April, 2005 from Zenit.Org, at http://www.catholiceducation.org/articles/politics/pg0143.html accessed 18 Nov. 2007.

Sacred Congregation For The Doctrine of The Faith, Declaration on Procured Abortion, Rome , 18 Nov 1974 S.21, at http://www.vatican.va/roman_curia/congregations/cfaith/documents/rc_con_cfaith_doc_19741118_declaration-abortion_en.html , accessed 21 April 2009.

Saeed, Abdullah, *Muslim Australians: Their Beliefs, Practices and Institutions*, Canberra, Commonwealth of Australia (Department of Immigration and Multicultural and Indigenous Affairs and Australian Multicultural Foundation in association with the University of Melbourne), 2004.

Said, Edward W, *Orientalism*, London, Penguin Books, 1991.

Smyth, Paul, 'Reclaiming community? From welfare society to welfare state in Australian Catholic social thought', *The Australian Journal of Politics and History* No.49, March 2003, pp.17ss.

Stark, Rodney, *The Victory of Reason: How Christianity Led to Freedom, Capitalism and Western Success,* New York, Random House, 2005.

Steinback, Udo, (Trans: Isabel Cole), 'Euro-Islam: One Word, Two Concepts, Lots of Problems.' *Qantara* 18 May 2005. <http://www.qantara.de/webcom/show article.php/ e-478/i.html>. accessed 10 June 2005.

Tamimi, Azzam, *Rachid Ghannouchi: A Democrat Within Islamism,* New York, Oxford University Press , 2001.

Tamimi, Azzam, 'Democracy in Islamic Political Thought', a lecture at Belfast Mosque, Northern Ireland, 1997 at http://www.iol.ie/~afifi/Articles/democracy.htm, accessed 30 July 2009.

Taylor, Charles, *Varieties of Religion Today, William James Revisited.* Cambridge, Mass., Harvard University Press, 2002.

Ward, Benedicta & Evans, GR, 'The Medieval West', in Hastings, 1999.

Warraq, Ibn (ed.), *The Quest for the Historical Muhammad,* New York, Prometheus Books, 2000.

Watt, W Montgomery, *Islamic Political Thought, The basic concepts,* Edinburgh University Press, 1968.

Weber, Max, *The Protestant Ethic and the Spirit of Capitalism,* New York & London, Routledge Classics, 2001.

Woods Jr., Thomas E, *How the Catholic Church Built Western Civilization,* Washington, Regnery Publishing, Inc., 2005.